50 Delicious Fruit Dishes for Home

By: Kelly Johnson

Table of Contents

- Fruit Salad
- Berry Parfait
- Mango Sticky Rice
- Apple Crumble
- Peach Cobbler
- Banana Pancakes
- Pineapple Fried Rice
- Strawberry Shortcake
- Watermelon Gazpacho
- Mixed Berry Smoothie
- Grilled Peaches with Honey
- Coconut Mango Chia Pudding
- Fig and Goat Cheese Tart
- Lemon Sorbet
- Avocado and Mango Salsa
- Raspberry Almond Tart
- Blueberry Muffins
- Pomegranate Glazed Chicken
- Pear and Gorgonzola Salad
- Cranberry Sauce
- Kiwi and Yogurt Bowl
- Cherry Clafoutis
- Grapefruit Brûlée
- Passionfruit Cheesecake
- Plum Galette
- Orange and Beet Salad
- Baked Apples with Cinnamon
- Mulberry Jam
- Papaya and Shrimp Salad
- Chocolate Dipped Strawberries
- Tropical Fruit Skewers
- Blackberry Cobbler
- Caramelized Pineapple Tarts
- Dragon Fruit Smoothie Bowl
- Melon Prosciutto Appetizer

- Rhubarb and Strawberry Pie
- Frozen Grape Snack
- Guava Pastry
- Lychee and Coconut Jelly
- Starfruit and Citrus Salad
- Persimmon Pudding
- Grapes and Cheese Platter
- Date and Walnut Bread
- Fig and Honey Yogurt
- Baked Plantains
- Mango Lassi
- Watermelon Feta Salad
- Roasted Pears with Cinnamon
- Apricot Glazed Salmon
- Spiced Apple Cider

Fruit Salad

Ingredients:

- 1 cup strawberries, hulled and halved
- 1 cup blueberries
- 1 cup grapes, halved
- 1 cup pineapple, diced
- 1 cup mango, diced
- 1 banana, sliced
- 1 tbsp honey
- 1 tbsp lime juice
- Fresh mint leaves for garnish

Instructions:

1. Combine all fruits in a large bowl.
2. Drizzle with honey and lime juice, then toss gently.
3. Garnish with mint leaves and serve.

Berry Parfait

Ingredients:

- 1 cup Greek yogurt
- ½ cup granola
- ½ cup mixed berries (strawberries, blueberries, raspberries)
- 1 tbsp honey

Instructions:

1. Layer yogurt, granola, and berries in a glass.
2. Repeat layers and drizzle with honey.
3. Serve immediately.

Mango Sticky Rice

Ingredients:

- 1 cup glutinous rice
- 1 cup coconut milk
- ⅓ cup sugar
- ¼ tsp salt
- 1 ripe mango, sliced
- 1 tbsp toasted sesame seeds

Instructions:

1. Rinse and soak rice for 2 hours, then steam until tender.
2. Heat coconut milk with sugar and salt until dissolved.
3. Mix half of the coconut milk with rice and let sit for 10 minutes.
4. Serve with sliced mango and drizzle remaining coconut milk.
5. Sprinkle sesame seeds on top.

Apple Crumble

Ingredients:

- 4 apples, peeled and sliced
- ¼ cup sugar
- 1 tsp cinnamon
- ½ cup flour
- ½ cup oats
- ¼ cup brown sugar
- ¼ cup butter, melted

Instructions:

1. Preheat oven to 350°F (175°C).
2. Toss apples with sugar and cinnamon, place in a baking dish.
3. Mix flour, oats, brown sugar, and butter until crumbly.
4. Sprinkle over apples and bake for 30 minutes.

Peach Cobbler

Ingredients:

- 4 cups sliced peaches
- ½ cup sugar
- 1 cup flour
- 1 tsp baking powder
- ½ tsp salt
- ½ cup milk
- ¼ cup butter, melted

Instructions:

1. Preheat oven to 375°F (190°C).
2. Toss peaches with sugar and place in a baking dish.
3. Mix flour, baking powder, salt, and milk, then pour over peaches.
4. Drizzle melted butter and bake for 40 minutes.

Banana Pancakes

Ingredients:

- 1 cup flour
- 1 tbsp sugar
- 1 tsp baking powder
- ½ tsp cinnamon
- 1 cup milk
- 1 ripe banana, mashed
- 1 egg
- 1 tsp vanilla extract

Instructions:

1. Mix dry ingredients in one bowl and wet ingredients in another.
2. Combine both and stir until smooth.
3. Cook pancakes on a greased pan over medium heat.
4. Flip when bubbles appear, then cook another minute.

Pineapple Fried Rice

Ingredients:

- 2 cups cooked rice
- 1 cup pineapple chunks
- ½ cup diced bell peppers
- ½ cup peas
- 2 eggs, scrambled
- 2 tbsp soy sauce
- 1 tbsp sesame oil
- 2 green onions, chopped

Instructions:

1. Heat sesame oil in a pan and stir-fry pineapple, peppers, and peas.
2. Add rice and soy sauce, stir well.
3. Push rice aside, scramble eggs, then mix everything together.
4. Garnish with green onions and serve.

Strawberry Shortcake

Ingredients:

- 2 cups flour
- ¼ cup sugar
- 1 tbsp baking powder
- ½ tsp salt
- ½ cup butter, cubed
- ¾ cup milk
- 1 cup whipped cream
- 2 cups strawberries, sliced

Instructions:

1. Preheat oven to 400°F (200°C).
2. Mix flour, sugar, baking powder, and salt.
3. Cut in butter, then add milk to form a dough.
4. Bake in 2-inch rounds for 15 minutes.
5. Layer with strawberries and whipped cream.

Watermelon Gazpacho

Ingredients:

- 3 cups watermelon, cubed
- 1 cucumber, diced
- ½ red bell pepper, diced
- ¼ red onion, diced
- 1 tbsp lime juice
- 1 tbsp olive oil
- Salt and pepper to taste

Instructions:

1. Blend half of the watermelon, cucumber, and bell pepper.
2. Stir in remaining diced ingredients.
3. Season with lime juice, olive oil, salt, and pepper.
4. Chill before serving.

Mixed Berry Smoothie

Ingredients:

- 1 cup mixed berries
- 1 banana
- 1 cup milk or yogurt
- 1 tbsp honey

Instructions:

1. Blend all ingredients until smooth.
2. Pour into a glass and serve.

Grilled Peaches with Honey

Ingredients:

- 2 peaches, halved and pitted
- 1 tbsp honey
- 1 tbsp butter, melted

Instructions:

1. Brush peaches with melted butter.
2. Grill cut-side down for 3 minutes.
3. Drizzle with honey before serving.

Coconut Mango Chia Pudding

Ingredients:

- 1 cup coconut milk
- ¼ cup chia seeds
- 1 tbsp honey
- ½ cup mango, diced

Instructions:

1. Mix coconut milk, chia seeds, and honey in a bowl.
2. Refrigerate for at least 4 hours, stirring occasionally.
3. Top with diced mango before serving.

Fig and Goat Cheese Tart

Ingredients:

- 1 sheet puff pastry
- ½ cup goat cheese
- 6 fresh figs, sliced
- 1 tbsp honey
- 1 tsp fresh thyme

Instructions:

1. Preheat oven to 375°F (190°C).
2. Roll out puff pastry and spread goat cheese on top.
3. Arrange fig slices and drizzle with honey.
4. Sprinkle thyme and bake for 20 minutes.

Lemon Sorbet

Ingredients:

- 1 cup lemon juice
- ½ cup sugar
- 1 cup water
- 1 tbsp lemon zest

Instructions:

1. Heat water and sugar until dissolved, then cool.
2. Mix with lemon juice and zest.
3. Freeze, stirring every 30 minutes until set.

Avocado and Mango Salsa

Ingredients:

- 1 avocado, diced
- 1 mango, diced
- ½ red onion, finely chopped
- 1 tbsp lime juice
- 1 tbsp cilantro, chopped
- Salt to taste

Instructions:

1. Combine all ingredients in a bowl.
2. Toss gently and serve fresh.

Raspberry Almond Tart

Ingredients:

- 1 pie crust
- ½ cup raspberry jam
- ½ cup sliced almonds
- 1 tbsp powdered sugar

Instructions:

1. Preheat oven to 350°F (175°C).
2. Spread raspberry jam over crust.
3. Sprinkle almonds and bake for 20 minutes.
4. Dust with powdered sugar before serving.

Blueberry Muffins

Ingredients:

- 2 cups flour
- ½ cup sugar
- 1 tsp baking powder
- ½ tsp salt
- 1 cup milk
- 1 egg
- ½ cup butter, melted
- 1 cup blueberries

Instructions:

1. Preheat oven to 375°F (190°C).
2. Mix dry ingredients in one bowl and wet ingredients in another.
3. Combine both and fold in blueberries.
4. Fill muffin cups and bake for 20 minutes.

Pomegranate Glazed Chicken

Ingredients:

- 2 chicken breasts
- ½ cup pomegranate juice
- 2 tbsp honey
- 1 tbsp soy sauce

Instructions:

1. Heat pomegranate juice, honey, and soy sauce until thickened.
2. Grill chicken, basting with glaze until cooked.

Pear and Gorgonzola Salad

Ingredients:

- 4 cups mixed greens
- 1 pear, sliced
- ¼ cup crumbled Gorgonzola
- ¼ cup walnuts
- 2 tbsp balsamic dressing

Instructions:

1. Toss all ingredients together in a bowl.
2. Drizzle with balsamic dressing and serve.

Cranberry Sauce

Ingredients:

- 2 cups cranberries
- ½ cup sugar
- ½ cup orange juice

Instructions:

1. Simmer all ingredients until cranberries burst.
2. Cool before serving.

Kiwi and Yogurt Bowl

Ingredients:

- 1 cup Greek yogurt
- 1 kiwi, sliced
- 1 tbsp honey
- ¼ cup granola

Instructions:

1. Layer yogurt, kiwi, and granola in a bowl.
2. Drizzle with honey before serving.

Cherry Clafoutis

Ingredients:

- 2 cups cherries, pitted
- ½ cup flour
- ½ cup sugar
- 1 cup milk
- 3 eggs
- 1 tsp vanilla extract

Instructions:

1. Preheat oven to 375°F (190°C).
2. Whisk flour, sugar, milk, eggs, and vanilla into a batter.
3. Pour over cherries in a greased dish.
4. Bake for 30 minutes until golden.

Grapefruit Brûlée

Ingredients:

- 1 grapefruit, halved
- 2 tbsp sugar

Instructions:

1. Sprinkle sugar evenly over the cut sides of the grapefruit.
2. Use a kitchen torch to caramelize the sugar until golden and bubbly.
3. Let cool slightly before serving.

Passionfruit Cheesecake

Ingredients:

- 1 ½ cups graham cracker crumbs
- ½ cup butter, melted
- 16 oz cream cheese, softened
- ½ cup sugar
- 2 eggs
- ½ cup passionfruit pulp

Instructions:

1. Preheat oven to 325°F (163°C).
2. Mix crumbs and butter, then press into a baking dish.
3. Beat cream cheese, sugar, eggs, and passionfruit until smooth.
4. Pour over crust and bake for 40 minutes.
5. Chill before serving.

Plum Galette

Ingredients:

- 1 pie crust
- 4 plums, sliced
- ¼ cup sugar
- 1 tbsp cornstarch
- 1 egg, beaten

Instructions:

1. Preheat oven to 375°F (190°C).
2. Toss plums with sugar and cornstarch.
3. Place fruit in the center of the crust, fold edges over.
4. Brush crust with egg wash and bake for 30 minutes.

Orange and Beet Salad

Ingredients:

- 2 oranges, segmented
- 2 roasted beets, sliced
- 4 cups arugula
- ¼ cup feta cheese, crumbled
- 2 tbsp balsamic dressing

Instructions:

1. Toss all ingredients in a bowl.
2. Drizzle with balsamic dressing before serving.

Baked Apples with Cinnamon

Ingredients:

- 4 apples, cored
- ¼ cup brown sugar
- 1 tsp cinnamon
- 2 tbsp butter

Instructions:

1. Preheat oven to 375°F (190°C).
2. Mix sugar and cinnamon, then fill apple cores with mixture.
3. Top with butter and bake for 30 minutes.

Mulberry Jam

Ingredients:

- 2 cups mulberries
- 1 cup sugar
- 1 tbsp lemon juice

Instructions:

1. Simmer mulberries, sugar, and lemon juice over low heat.
2. Stir frequently until thickened, about 20 minutes.
3. Cool and store in a jar.

Papaya and Shrimp Salad

Ingredients:

- 1 ripe papaya, julienned
- ½ lb cooked shrimp
- ½ cup cherry tomatoes, halved
- 2 tbsp lime juice
- 1 tbsp fish sauce
- 1 tbsp peanuts, crushed

Instructions:

1. Toss all ingredients together in a bowl.
2. Serve fresh.

Chocolate Dipped Strawberries

Ingredients:

- 1 cup chocolate chips
- 12 strawberries

Instructions:

1. Melt chocolate chips in a microwave or double boiler.
2. Dip strawberries and place on parchment paper.
3. Chill until chocolate hardens.

Tropical Fruit Skewers

Ingredients:

- 1 mango, cubed
- 1 pineapple, cubed
- 1 banana, sliced
- 1 kiwi, sliced
- ½ cup shredded coconut

Instructions:

1. Thread fruit onto skewers.
2. Sprinkle with shredded coconut before serving.

Blackberry Cobbler

Ingredients:

- 3 cups blackberries
- ½ cup sugar
- 1 cup flour
- 1 tsp baking powder
- ½ cup butter, melted
- ½ cup milk

Instructions:

1. Preheat oven to 375°F (190°C).
2. Mix blackberries and sugar in a baking dish.
3. Combine flour, baking powder, butter, and milk into a batter.
4. Pour over blackberries and bake for 40 minutes.

Caramelized Pineapple Tarts

Ingredients:

- 1 sheet puff pastry
- 1 cup pineapple, diced
- ¼ cup brown sugar
- 1 tbsp butter
- 1 tsp cinnamon

Instructions:

1. Preheat oven to 375°F (190°C).
2. Cook pineapple, sugar, butter, and cinnamon in a pan until caramelized.
3. Cut puff pastry into squares, place pineapple in the center, and fold edges.
4. Bake for 15-20 minutes until golden brown.

Dragon Fruit Smoothie Bowl

Ingredients:

- 1 cup dragon fruit, cubed
- 1 frozen banana
- ½ cup coconut milk
- ½ cup granola
- ¼ cup sliced kiwi and berries

Instructions:

1. Blend dragon fruit, banana, and coconut milk until smooth.
2. Pour into a bowl and top with granola, kiwi, and berries.

Melon Prosciutto Appetizer

Ingredients:

- 1 cantaloupe, cubed
- 8 slices prosciutto
- ½ cup fresh basil leaves
- ¼ cup balsamic glaze

Instructions:

1. Wrap prosciutto around melon cubes.
2. Garnish with basil and drizzle with balsamic glaze.

Rhubarb and Strawberry Pie

Ingredients:

- 1 pie crust
- 2 cups rhubarb, chopped
- 2 cups strawberries, sliced
- ¾ cup sugar
- ¼ cup cornstarch
- 1 egg, beaten

Instructions:

1. Preheat oven to 375°F (190°C).
2. Toss rhubarb and strawberries with sugar and cornstarch.
3. Pour into crust, cover with top crust, and brush with egg wash.
4. Bake for 40-45 minutes.

Frozen Grape Snack

Ingredients:

- 2 cups grapes
- ½ cup Greek yogurt
- ¼ cup honey

Instructions:

1. Dip grapes in yogurt, drizzle with honey, and freeze for 2 hours.

Guava Pastry

Ingredients:

- 1 sheet puff pastry
- ½ cup guava paste
- ¼ cup cream cheese
- 1 egg, beaten

Instructions:

1. Preheat oven to 375°F (190°C).
2. Cut puff pastry into squares and fill with guava paste and cream cheese.
3. Fold, seal, brush with egg wash, and bake for 15-20 minutes.

Lychee and Coconut Jelly

Ingredients:

- 1 can lychees, drained
- 1 cup coconut milk
- 2 tbsp sugar
- 1 tbsp gelatin

Instructions:

1. Heat coconut milk and sugar until warm.
2. Dissolve gelatin in warm mixture and pour into molds.
3. Add lychees and chill until set.

Starfruit and Citrus Salad

Ingredients:

- 1 starfruit, sliced
- 1 orange, segmented
- ½ grapefruit, segmented
- ¼ cup pomegranate seeds
- 1 tbsp honey

Instructions:

1. Toss all ingredients together in a bowl.
2. Drizzle with honey before serving.

Persimmon Pudding

Ingredients:

- 2 ripe persimmons, mashed
- ½ cup sugar
- 1 cup flour
- ½ tsp cinnamon
- ½ cup milk
- 1 egg, beaten

Instructions:

1. Preheat oven to 350°F (175°C).
2. Mix all ingredients until smooth and pour into a greased dish.
3. Bake for 35-40 minutes.

Grapes and Cheese Platter

Ingredients:

- 1 cup grapes
- ½ cup assorted cheeses
- ¼ cup nuts
- Crackers or bread

Instructions:

1. Arrange all ingredients on a platter.
2. Serve with crackers or bread.

Date and Walnut Bread

Ingredients:

- 1 ½ cups flour
- ½ cup chopped dates
- ½ cup chopped walnuts
- ½ cup sugar
- 1 tsp baking soda
- ½ tsp salt
- ¾ cup milk
- 1 egg
- ¼ cup melted butter

Instructions:

1. Preheat oven to 350°F (175°C).
2. Mix dry ingredients, then add milk, egg, and butter. Stir well.
3. Pour into a greased loaf pan and bake for 45-50 minutes.

Fig and Honey Yogurt

Ingredients:

- 1 cup Greek yogurt
- 3 fresh figs, sliced
- 1 tbsp honey
- ¼ cup granola

Instructions:

1. Layer yogurt, figs, and granola in a bowl.
2. Drizzle with honey before serving.

Baked Plantains

Ingredients:

- 2 ripe plantains, sliced
- 1 tbsp coconut oil
- 1 tbsp brown sugar
- ½ tsp cinnamon

Instructions:

1. Preheat oven to 375°F (190°C).
2. Toss plantains with coconut oil, sugar, and cinnamon.
3. Bake for 20 minutes, flipping halfway.

Mango Lassi

Ingredients:

- 1 ripe mango, peeled and diced
- 1 cup yogurt
- ½ cup milk
- 1 tbsp honey
- ¼ tsp cardamom

Instructions:

1. Blend all ingredients until smooth.
2. Serve chilled.

Watermelon Feta Salad

Ingredients:

- 2 cups watermelon, cubed
- ½ cup feta cheese, crumbled
- ¼ cup fresh mint leaves
- 1 tbsp balsamic glaze

Instructions:

1. Toss watermelon and feta together.
2. Garnish with mint and drizzle with balsamic glaze.

Roasted Pears with Cinnamon

Ingredients:

- 2 pears, halved
- 1 tbsp honey
- ½ tsp cinnamon
- ¼ cup chopped walnuts

Instructions:

1. Preheat oven to 375°F (190°C).
2. Drizzle pears with honey, sprinkle with cinnamon and walnuts.
3. Bake for 20 minutes.

Apricot Glazed Salmon

Ingredients:

- 2 salmon fillets
- ¼ cup apricot preserves
- 1 tbsp soy sauce
- 1 tbsp Dijon mustard
- ½ tsp garlic powder

Instructions:

1. Preheat oven to 400°F (200°C).
2. Mix preserves, soy sauce, mustard, and garlic powder.
3. Brush onto salmon and bake for 12-15 minutes.

Spiced Apple Cider

Ingredients:

- 4 cups apple cider
- 1 cinnamon stick
- 3 cloves
- 1 star anise
- 1 tbsp honey

Instructions:

1. Heat all ingredients in a saucepan over medium heat.
2. Simmer for 10 minutes, then strain and serve warm.